A Crabtree Branches Book

SERVING with Honor

AIR FORCE

written by Bernard Conaghan

Crabtree Publishing

crabtreebooks.com

School-to-Home Support for Caregivers and Teachers

This high-interest book is designed to motivate striving students with engaging topics while building fluency, vocabulary, and an interest in reading. Here are a few questions and activities to help the reader build upon his or her comprehension skills.

Before Reading:

- *What do I think this book is about?*
- *What do I know about this topic?*
- *What do I want to learn about this topic?*
- *Why am I reading this book?*

During Reading:

- *I wonder why...*
- *I'm curious to know...*
- *How is this like something I already know?*
- *What have I learned so far?*

After Reading:

- *What was the author trying to teach me?*
- *What are some details?*
- *How did the photographs and captions help me understand more?*
- *Read the book again and look for the vocabulary words.*
- *What questions do I still have?*

Extension Activities:

- *What was your favorite part of the book? Write a paragraph on it.*
- *Draw a picture of your favorite thing you learned from the book.*

Table of Contents

1: Mission 4

2: Values 6

3: Uniform 10

4: Equipment and Vehicles 12

5: Training 16

6: Careers 20

7: Ways to Serve 24

8: Showing Appreciation 28

9: Glossary 30

10: Index 31

11: Websites to Visit 31

12: About the Author 32

Mission

The United States Air Force is one branch of the United States Armed Forces. It is responsible for **military operations** in the air to keep the U.S. safe.

Values

Airmen are expected to live by values. They are: **integrity** first, service before self, and excellence in all we do. The three core Air Force values guide airmen's actions every day, whether on or off the job. The Airman's Creed is an **oath** to these values.

Air Force
Medal of Honor

Fun Fact

The U.S. Medal of Honor is the country's highest military award. It is given to airmen who show courage and bravery while risking their lives.

Every service member must say the Oath of Enlistment. Officers say the military oath of office. This is a promise to defend the **U.S. Constitution**.

FOR LEASE
FOR LEASE

Uniform

The Air Force has strict rules for uniforms. Combat uniforms have **camouflage** and are easy to work in. Service uniforms have a button-up shirt and are worn every day. Pilots wear flight suits. Dress or "mess" uniforms are the most formal. These are worn on special occasions.

Fun Fact

Air Force dress blues have silver-colored buttons with Hap Arnold wings, the insignia, or symbol, of the Air Force.

Equipment and Vehicles

The Air Force uses planes to accomplish their **mission** of fly, fight, and win. The F-15 Eagle is the main fighter jet. Helicopters like the HH-60G Pave Hawk are used for search and rescue missions during combat.

HH-60G Pave Hawk

F-15C Eagle

Some planes are used for special purposes. Radar planes find vehicles in the air, on land, and in the sea. Hurricane hunters use the Lockheed WC-130J. The U.S. president flies in Air Force One.

WC-130J Super Hercules

Air Force One

Fun Fact

Fighter jets have ejection seats that pilots use to escape the plane in the air. The seat has a parachute that is used to return safely to the ground.

Air Force pilots use special equipment. Night vision goggles help them see in the dark. Finger lights turn the pilot's fingertips into flashlights. The **G suit** keeps them from losing consciousness at extreme speeds.

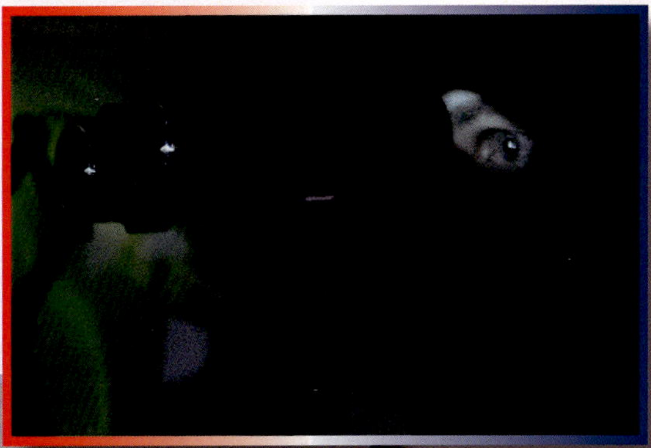

Training

Airmen must be strong and ready for missions. Basic Military Training (BMT) is the first type of training. How to work as a team, discipline, and the three core Air Force values are learned. BMT lasts about 8 ½ weeks.

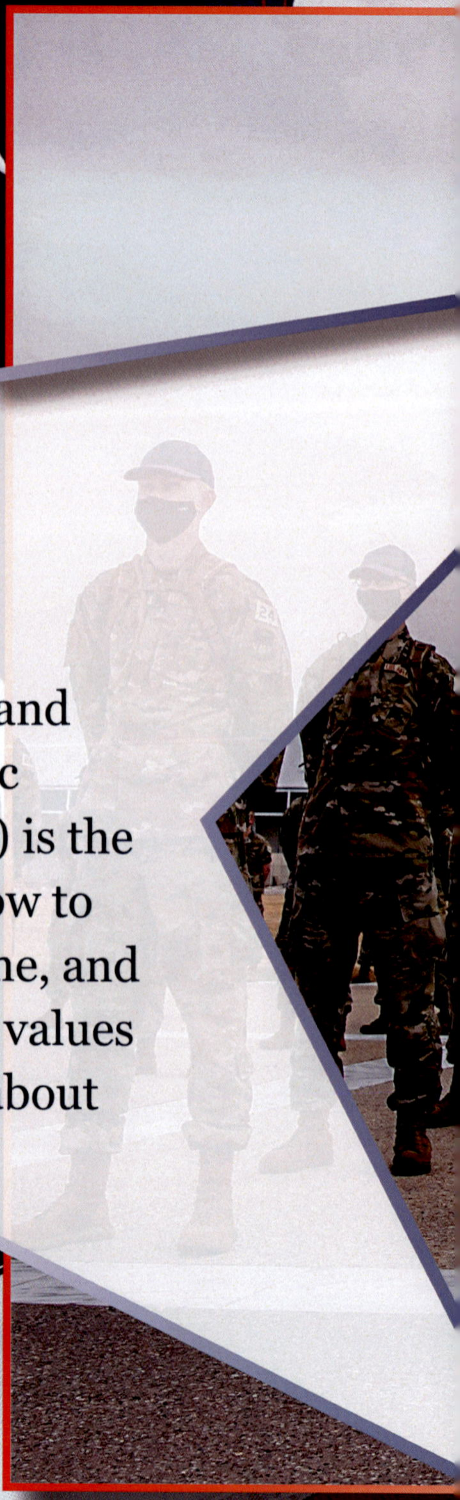

Advanced Individual Training (AIT) is next. Airmen learn the specific skills needed for their Air Force Specialty Code. Most technical training happens at bases in Texas or Mississippi.

Careers

The U.S. Air Force has many different types of jobs for the battlefield. The Air Battle Manager guides the pilots in battle just like a coach calls the plays in a game. Computer Systems Programming Specialists create programs to organize and show data.

Fun Fact

Many jobs in the Air Force prepare soldiers for jobs as ***civilians****. Some training allows soldiers to get a professional license from trade organizations.*

The U.S. Air Force also has jobs that provide support to the troops. Culinary specialists prepare and serve the food. Cargo specialists make sure that equipment, supplies, and mail arrive wherever the troops are located.

Keeping equipment working is important. Electronics specialists repair electronics and safely disarm explosives. Mechanics keep aircraft running.

Ways to Serve

There are three main ways to serve in the U.S. Air Force. Active duty airmen live and work on an Air Force base full-time. Airmen in the Air Force Reserve Command serve part-time and can live anywhere in the U.S. The Air National Guard also serve part-time. They can be called by the state or federal government.

Fun Fact

Air Force civilians are workers for the U.S. Air Force but are not airmen. Jobs include cybersecurity, medicine, office work, and support for families on base.

The Air Force has basic requirements to **enlist**. A person must be a U.S. citizen, between the ages of 17 and 39, and have a high school diploma. The Armed Services Vocational Aptitude Battery (ASVAB) tests a person's knowledge of reading, math, science, and thinking. A medical exam determines if a person is healthy and strong.

Showing Appreciation

Members of the Air Force are on call every day of the year. They put their lives at risk to keep us safe. We celebrate them throughout the year. May is Military Appreciation Month.

Thank You

HONORING ALL WHO SERVE

Veterans Day is a time to thank those who are serving. It is also for those who served in the past and are still living. Memorial Day is for remembering the men and women who lost their lives serving their country. Are you ready to serve in the U.S. Air Force?

Glossary

camouflage (**ka**·muh·flaazh) Disguising items to help someone blend in with their surroundings

civilian (suh·**vi**·lyn) Someone who is not in the armed forces or police

enlist (uhn·**list**) To join the armed forces

G suit (G Soot) A flight suit that adds pressure to the lower body to keep blood moving up to the brain

integrity (uhn·**teh**·gruh·tee) Having strong morals

military operations (**mi**·luh·teh·ree aa·pr·**ay**·shnz) Armed actions in response to a situation

mission (**mi**·shn) An assignment

oath (owth) A promise

U.S. Constitution (kaan·stuh·**too**·shn) The rights and laws that are the basis for the government of the United States

Index

Advanced Individual Training (AIT) 18
Air Force Specialty Code 18
Airman's Creed 6
Basic Military Training (BMT) 16
civilian 21, 22, 23, 25
F-15 Eagle 12
hurricane hunters 13
Memorial Day 29
Military Appreciation Month 28
Oath of Enlistment 8
Veterans Day 29

Websites to Visit

www.airforce.com
www.ang.af.mil
www.militaryonesource.mil

About the Author

Bernard Conaghan lives in South Carolina with his German shepherd named Duke. His grandmother was the jeep driver for the Major General for the U.S. Marines during World War II. He is a coach on his son's football team. He always eats one scoop of peach ice cream after dinner.

Crabtree Publishing

crabtreebooks.com 800-387-7650

Written by: Bernard Conaghan
Designed by: Jen Bowers
Proofreader: Petrice Custance
Production manager: Candice Campbell

Photographs: Cover U.S. Air Force photo, U.S. flag ©2008 J. Helgason/Shutterstock; p.3 U.S. Air Force photo/Senior Airman Koby Saunders; p.5 U.S. Air Force photo/2nd Lt. Mary Begy; p.6 U.S. Air Force photo/Master Sgt. Scott T. Sturkol; p.7 Arlington National Cemetery/public domain; p.9 U.S. Air Force photo/Tech. Sgt. Ryan Conroy; p.10 ©2010 Keith McIntyre/Shutterstock; p.11 U.S. Air Force photo; p.12 U.S. Air Force photo/Airman Thomas S. Keisler IV, U.S. Air Force photo/Senior Airman Zachary Bumpus; p.13 U.S. Air Force photo, U.S. Air National Guard photo/Tech. Sgt. Danielle Hopkins; p.14 U.S. Air Force photo; p.15 U.S. Air Force photo/Airman 1st Class Anthony Jennings, U.S. Air Force photo/Tech. Sgt. Daniel Asselta; p.17 U.S. Air Force photo/Trevor Cokley; p.19 U.S. Air Force photo/Airman 1st Class Jessica Sanchez-Chen; p.20 U.S. Air Force photo/Senior Airman Bryan Guthrie; p.21 U.S. Air Force photo; p.22 U.S. Air Force photo/Lan Kim; p.23 U.S. Air National Guard photo/Capt. Paul Stennett; p.25 U.S. Air Force photo/Airman 1st Class Melody Bordeaux; p.27 ©2019 smolaw/Shutterstock; p.28-29 Black Creator 24/Shutterstock

Published in Canada
Crabtree Publishing
616 Welland Avenue
St. Catharines, Ontario
L2M 5V6

Published in the United States
Crabtree Publishing
347 Fifth Avenue
Suite 1402-145
New York, NY 10016

Hardcover	978-1-0396-6034-2
Paperback	978-1-0396-6229-2
Ebook (pdf)	978-1-0396-7025-9
Epub	978-1-0396-7223-9
Read-along	978-1-0396-7421-9
Audio book	978-1-0396-7619-0

Library and Archives Canada Cataloguing in Publication
Available at the Library and Archives Canada

Library of Congress Cataloging-in-Publication Data
Available at the Library of Congress

Printed in the U.S.A./CP052026